For Johnny, whose questions became my questions.

www.hmhco.com
The text of this book is set in Avenir.

Library of Congress Cataloging-in-Publication Data

Names: Heos, Bridget, author.
Title: Shell, beak, tusk : shared traits and the wonders of adaptation / by Bridget Heos.
Description: Boston ; New York : Houghton Mifflin Harcourt, [2017] |
    Audience: Ages 6—9. | Audience: K to grade 3. | Includes bibliographical
    references.
Identifiers: LCCN 2016013090 | ISBN 9780544811669 (hardcover)
Subjects: LCSH: Convergence (Biology)—Juvenile literature. | Adaptation
    (Biology)—Juvenile literature. | Evolution—Juvenile literature.
Classification: LCC QH373 .H46 2017 | DDC 576.8—dc23 LC record available at https://lccn.
loc.gov/2016013090

ISBN 978-0-544-81166-9
Printed in China
SCP 10 9 8 7 6 5 4 3 2 1
4500638659

SHELL, BEAK, TUSK

Shared Traits and the Wonders of Adaptation

by Bridget Heos

Houghton Mifflin Harcourt

Boston   New York

TERRIFIC TRAITS

Every living thing on Earth has traits that allow it to eat or avoid being eaten. For instance, a sticky tongue allows an anteater to pick up ants. And a shell protects a turtle from a coyote. A sticky shell, on the other hand, would be inconvenient in both respects. Predators would stick to it, and the poor turtle would be forced to lug around dangerous animals while foraging for food! Thus, only helpful traits develop over time in a process called evolution.

Animals that are related often have similar traits, which they inherited from a common ancestor. Rabbits and hares both have long ears. Whales and dolphins both have fins. This is not surprising; you may have inherited traits from your relatives too: your grandmother's freckles or your uncle's ears. However, some animals share traits but are not related. Why? Because they have adapted the same traits separately in order to survive in their environments. This is called convergent evolution.

Think about it: If a sticky tongue helps one animal adapt to eating ants, wouldn't that same trait help an ant-eating animal across the globe? Both animals, separately, would be better equipped to survive and then pass the trait on to their babies. And so the same traits—such as shell, beak, and tusks—evolve over and over again in different animals.

SPINES ARE FOR PRICKING.

A porcupine's spines grow to a foot (30 centimeters) long. When the porcupine is scared, the spines stand straight out. If a coyote, lion, or owl makes the mistake of trying to eat the porcupine, they get pricked. Not only that, but some spines break off and stay stuck in the attacker.

The echidna is covered in spikes too. If it feels threatened, it curls up into a spiny ball. This tells its predators—mainly dingos and dogs—not to mess with it.

● ● ●

Though they share a spiky defense system, the porcupine and echidna live on opposite sides of the world and are not related. A porcupine, which lives everywhere but Australia and Antarctica, is part of the rodent family. Native to Australia, an echidna is a rare kind of mammal that lays eggs and is called a monotreme.

A SHELL IS FOR HIDING.

A turtle shell is made of bone. Most of the turtle's bones are inside its body. But its backbone and rib cage grow as the shell. If a box turtle sees a fox or raccoon, it hides its head, tail, and legs inside the bony shell. Unable to break through, the predator eventually gives up, and the turtle wins the game of hide-and-seek.

The only bony part of a snail is its shell. The rest of its body—the soft part—is called the foot. If a snail is threatened, it pulls its foot (which includes its head, belly, and everything else) inside the shell. Beetles, spiders, and even some larger animals like birds can't crack the shell, so the snail is safe.

● ● ●

The box turtle is a reptile related to lizards and snakes. A snail is part of the mollusk family, along with clams, oysters, and octopuses. Turtles and snails are not even distant cousins.

TALL EARS ARE FOR HEARING— AND MORE.

A rabbit's tall ears can rotate 270 degrees—or three quarters of the way around. This allows the rabbit to hear foxes, dogs, and hawks approach from any direction. The ears also cool the rabbit off in the summer and warm it up in the winter. During cold weather, blood vessels in the ears shrink, so that less warm blood flows to the ears and escapes through the skin. This keeps the heat inside the rabbit.

A bilby has tall ears for the same reason: to hear predators, which include pythons, dingos, and feral cats. In the hot Australian desert, the bilby may also use its ears to shed heat. In hot weather, blood vessels in the ears swell so that more warm blood travels there. For an animal with big ears, this allows plenty of warmth to escape through the skin.

● ● ●

Rabbits, which live all over the world, are rodents. Bilbies live only in Australia. They are marsupials like kangaroos. In addition to big ears, rabbits and bilbies both have strong hind legs for hopping away from predators.

WINGS ARE FOR FLYING.

A bird's wings are covered with stiff feathers. The feathers push down the air, and the air pushes back up. This allows the bird to fly. Flying makes birds better at catching prey, finding fruits and nuts, and escaping predators.

Bat wings are made not of feathers but cartilage. (Your ears are also made of cartilage.) It stretches from the bat's long fingers to its feet. Flying allows bats to hunt insects in midflight and to feast on many different plants in one night.

● ● ●

Birds and bats developed wings separately. Birds evolved from fast and ferocious dinosaurs called theropods, which included tyrannosaurs and raptors. Bats, which are mammals, likely evolved from a mammal that glided from tree to tree, just as lemurs and flying squirrels do today.

BLACK AND WHITE IS FOR CAMOUFLAGE.

Penguins may appear to be wearing tuxedos, but their color pattern is actually camouflage. A shark or seal swimming over a penguin will fail to see its black back, which blends in with the dark ocean depths. It's hard for them to see a penguin from underneath, too. Its white belly gets masked by the sunlight streaming in from above. If sharks and seals can't see a penguin, they can't eat it!

Orcas, or killer whales, are also black and white. But as the top predator in the ocean, an orca doesn't use its camouflage for protection. Rather, the orca's black and white pattern allows it to sneak up on the animals it eats, such as seals, whales, and even penguins (if the orca can see them!).

● ● ●

Though they share the ocean, a penguin is a bird and an orca is a mammal. They both developed black and white coloring as an adaptation to life in the ocean.

A LIGHT IS FOR DRAWING ATTENTION.

A firefly's glow is caused by a chemical inside its body. The flashing light is usually used to attract a mate. But fireflies don't always play fair. Some trick other species. In that case, a firefly will see a familiar flash and approach, only to get eaten by the trickster insect.

In the darkness of the deep sea, the anglerfish's light dangles from its dorsal fin. It glows because of light-up bacteria living inside the fish. The light lures other fish to come near. Then the anglerfish eats them.

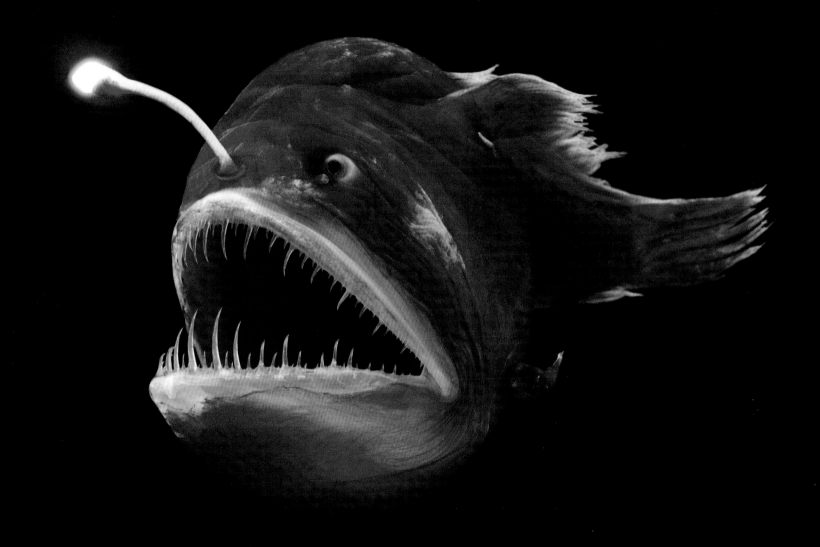

A firefly is a beetle, a type of insect. An anglerfish is, of course, a fish. In both cases, the lights say, "Look at me!" What they don't say is "I'm going to eat you!"

A BEAK IS FOR CRUSHING.

A parrot's beak is thick and sharp. For instance, a macaw weighs just two pounds, but the force of its bite is 167 pounds per inch. That's five times stronger than the bite of a deadly python. But the parrot doesn't eat other animals. It uses its beak to crush nuts and seeds.

While an octopus beak is just like a parrot's, the octopus crushes not nuts but crabs and mollusks with its beak. It is the only hard part of its body.

• • •

An octopus is a cephalopod that lives in all the world's oceans. A parrot is a bird that is native to Central and South America, Africa, India, Southeast Asia, and Australia. But they both have a beak to help them eat hard things.

A **BILL** IS FOR SLURPING.

A duck bill is round and flat. Along the edge, there is a comb. The duck scoops up animals such as insects, snails, and fish from the pond. Then it spits out mud and muck through the comb. A duck's bill is soft around the edges so that it can feel its food.

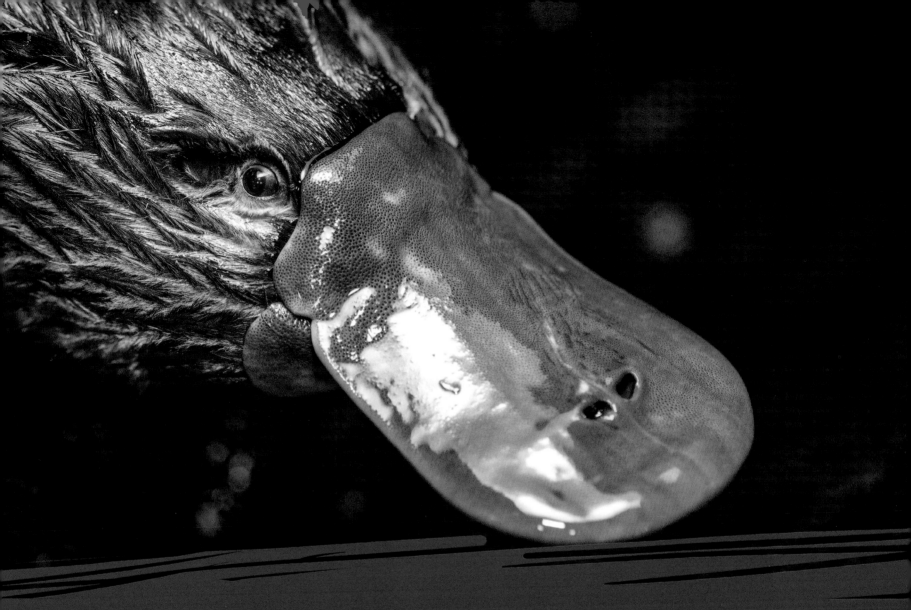

The duck-billed platypus uses its bill in the same way as a duck. The two animals also share webbed feet for paddling through the water. A platypus mother even lays eggs like a mother duck.

• • •

A duck is a bird, and a platypus is a mammal (a monotreme like the echidna). A platypus has fur, and once hatched, platypups drink milk from their mother. Fur and milk make a platypus a mammal, and not a duck.

A LONG STICKY TONGUE IS FOR CATCHING INSECTS.

A giant anteater's tongue is two feet (60 centimeters) long and super sticky. After clawing open an anthill and sticking its long snout inside, it begins flicking its tongue so that ants stick to it. In this way, it can eat 35,000 ants and termites each day!

● ● ●

Using its long, sticky tongue for the same purpose—to eat insects—is the aardvark. Its favorite food is termites, but it's been known to lick up its share of ants, too.

Anteaters and aardvarks are both mammals, but anteaters live in South America, and aardvarks, in Africa. The closest relative of the anteater is the sloth, whereas the aardvark is close cousins with the elephant.

A TUSK IS FOR . . . LOTS OF THINGS.

Walrus tusks are teeth that grow up to three feet (1 meter) long. Male walruses fight using their tusks. But the tusks are helpful in other ways too. When a walrus is swimming in the Arctic Sea and needs to take a breath, it can break through the ice with its tusks. A swimming walrus can also pull itself onto the ice with its tusks.

Elephant tusks are teeth too, but can grow to ten feet (3 meters) long. Like walruses, male elephants fight with their tusks. But elephants also use their tusks to dig for food and tear bark from trees, which they then eat.

● ● ●

Walruses and elephants are both mammals, but they are not close kin. A walrus's nearest relatives are sea lions and seals. Surprisingly, an elephant's closest cousin is also a sea creature: the manatee. Tusks are helpful tools for both walruses and elephants.

TWIN TRAITS

Helpful traits repeat themselves again and again in nature. In fact, when scientists discover new species, they often name them after animals they resemble. For instance, the mole cricket got its name because its forelegs look like a mole's, which it uses to dig underground just like its namesake. There are also animals known as the giraffe weevil (an insect with a long neck like a giraffe's), a porcupinefish (with spines like a porcupine's that stick out when it is threatened), and a parrotfish, which has a beaklike mouth similar to a parrot's. All of these animals developed twin traits because they needed them to survive similar situations—albeit often in very different environments. There are still animals that have yet to be discovered, and because of convergent evolution, they'll likely have features we've seen elsewhere. It's fun to imagine what these animals might be . . . A duck-billed lizard? An elephant-fish with tusks? Odd as they may seem, they will also look vaguely familiar!

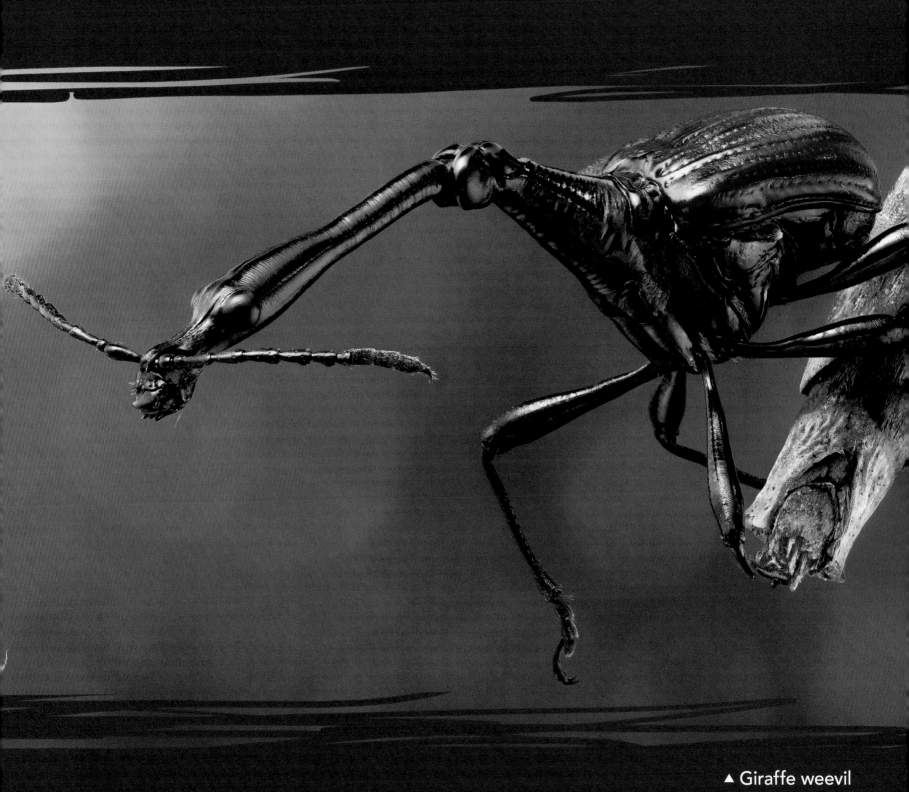

▲ Giraffe weevil

BIBLIOGRAPHY

Arizona State University School of Life Sciences. "Human, Bird, and Bat Bone Comparison." *Ask a Biologist*. askabiologist.asu.edu/human-bird-and-bat-bone-comparison

Barr, Brady. "Bite Force II." *Dangerous Encounters*. National Geographic Channel. Aired April 30, 2007.

Bradford, Alina. "Walrus Facts." *Live Science*. November 21, 2014. www.livescience.com/27442-walrus-facts.html

Caniglia, Guido. "Mechanistic Realization of the Turtle Shell." The Embryo Project Encyclopedia. October 10, 2011. embryo.asu.edu/pages/mechanistic-realization-turtle-shell

Davis, Brian. "The Scoop on Duck Bills." Ducks.org. www.ducks.org/conservation/waterfowl-biology/the-scoop-on-duck-bills

"Extreme Mammals." Chicago Field Museum exhibit. May 25, 2012–January 6, 2013.

Gorog, Toni, and Phil Myers. "New World Porcupines." Animal Diversity Web. animaldiversity.ummz.umich.edu/accounts/Erethizontidae

Horne, Francis. "How Are Seashells Created? Or Any Other Shell, Such as a Snail's or a Turtle's?" *Scientific American*. www.scientificamerican.com/article/how-are-seashells-created

Humble, Gary. "The Secret Life of a Bilby." ABC Science. April 6, 2006. www.abc.net.au/science/articles/2006/04/06/2042654.htm

Hutchinson, John R. "Vertebrate Flight." www.ucmp.berkeley.edu/vertebrates/flight/enter.html

Lloyd, John, and John Mitchinson. *The Book of Animal Ignorance*. New York: Random House, 2007.

McGhee, George. *Convergent Evolution: Limited Forms Most Beautiful*. Cambridge, Mass.: MIT Press, 2011.

National Geographic. "African Elephant." animals.nationalgeographic.com/animals/mammals/african-elephant

National Geographic. "Walrus." animals.nationalgeographic.com/animals/mammals/walrus

National Geographic Animals. animals.nationalgeographic.com

Niedzielski, Steven. "Florida Box Turtle." Animal Diversity Web. animaldiversity.ummz.umich.edu/site/accounts/information/Terrapene_carolina.html

Nordsieck, Robert. The Living World of Mollusks. www.molluscs.at/gastropoda/terrestrial

Palmer, Douglas. *Evolution: The Story of Life*. Berkeley: University of California Press, 2009.

Parks & Wildlife Service Tasmania. "Short-Beaked Echidna, Tachyglossus Aculeatus." www.parks.tas.gov.au/?base=4796

PBS. *The Living Edens: Etosha*. www.pbs.org-edens-etosha-elephant.htm

Reeves, Randall, Brent Stewart, Phillip Clapham, James Powell. Ill. by Pieter Folkens. *Guide to Marine Mammals of the World.* New York: Knopf, 2002.

Rickel, Jana. "Rabbit Ears: A Structural Look . . . Injury or Disease Can Send Your Rabbit into a Spin." House Rabbit Society. www.rabbit.org/journal/4-11/ear.html

University of California Museum of Paleontology. "A Light in the Darkness," in "A Fisheye View of the Tree of Life." Understanding Evolution. evolution.berkeley.edu/evolibrary/article/fishtree_05

University of Illinois at Urbana-Champaign Department of Physics. "How Do Birds Fly?" October 22, 2007. van.physics.illinois.edu/qa/listing.php?id=760

Zimmer, Carl. "Blink Twice If You Like Me." *New York Times,* June 29, 2009. www.nytimes.com/2009/06/30/science/30firefly.html?pagewanted=all&_r=0

Zimmermann, Kim Ann. "Brachiosaurus: Facts About the Giraffe-like Dinosaur." Live Science. November 26, 2012. www.livescience.com/25222-ankylosaurus.html

PHOTO CREDITS

INDEX